Attack of the Bear Market!
(How Anyone Can Invest in Crypto-Currency – 3rd Edition)

By D.M. Brooks

Preface

Chapter 1: Crypto Background

Chapter 2: What is Crypto-Currency?

Chapter 3: How is Crypto-Currency Used?

Chapter 4: Taxes and Crypto

Chapter 5: Crypto Trading Strategies

Chapter 6: Waking Up to Reality

Chapter 7: Additional Resources

Chapter 8: Summary – Good Luck!

Preface

Since writing the first two editions of my How Anyone Can Invest series, I have seen the stages of a market cycle up close and personally. What began as a dream come true – being an early adopter in an investment boom cycle – ended with nearly all book sales, twitter follows, interest from friends and my investments deflated and disillusioned. As I write this, investments have not returned to their previous highs and we have endured 10 months of decline and sideways trading.

Amid these market conditions, why write another book? Well, what better time than during a bear market to help other investors and enthusiasts? **Actually, Bear markets can be a good thi**

Yes, the profits dry up and the speculation isn't driving up new highs overnight in your favorite investment, but this is the time where fortunes can be made by continuing to buy the dip and increasing your investment for cheap!

The Bear market can be brutal

Remember how exuberant we all were at the end of 2017 about crypto? Remember the general sentiment about how 2018 was going to melt everyone's face off? We all dreamed of rocketing to the moon in our crypto-powered Lamborghinis.

Oops.

Yeah, 2018 has been that kind of year; rough, full of losses and bloody to trade most cryptocurrency in.

Sometimes it's best to take a break from the daily angst when the market has yet to fully capitulate and rebuild.

Let's not overreact to today's crypto market

Before delving entirely into this topic, let's pull back and take a macro view of cryptocurrency as a technology.

Despite this down year, we are still on the cusp of either widespread acceptance of Bitcoin, a compelling use case for Ethereum d-apps, or a mainstream breakthrough for everyday small and quick transactions. To date none of this has really happened yet on a large scale for the mainstream consumer. (I know XRP/Ripple has a ton of banking adoptions this year).

However, it is important to continually pull back the lens, refresh your intuitions and look at this from the perspective of early adoption periods (like 1990's Internet). Bitcoin has only been around since 2009 and it has seen rapid growth over the past 3 years. Prior to then, the momentum was steady, but it was slow and filled with down months. All crypto-coins have taken awhile to gain value, despite a few explosions; the general trend is a slow climb up over years.

This market cycle is normal

This slow climb over the years is what I base my bullish projections on and why this book isn't going to spread any fear of the unknown. The crypto market and technology simply is relevant and is only going to continue to grow.

If you believe in blockchain technology, in decentralized currency or in the advantages that crypto-currency brings to consumers, you have a compelling reason to invest with a long-term strategy and view.

Remember – This is the natural technological progression of currency from rocks to minerals to paper to digital. It's coming regardless of what people say today. The only question is who will be there early enough to make large profits from it?

If you've followed along and have money in crypto so far, then you are an early adopter who can make money in crypto markets as the cycles continue. Even with the downturn, you can still position yourself very well for future rewards.

Avoiding mistakes of the past

Cycles are painful as often or more than they are pleasant.

Most people will give up or call it all a scam since they didn't follow the principles of Technical Analysis to protect themselves from selling at the bottom or buying at the top. This is the biggest mistake I have seen people make in stocks and now crypto-coins!

They will see Bitcoin approaching $10,500 during the euphoria stage and go all-in, then when it drops down to $5900, they will sell based off of fear, unknown and doubt (FUD). When trading anything dealing in markets, you must always maintain your sobriety and never let emotions get in the way of a good trade.

I've found that keeping a journal with reasons for each trade (where I have to justify it to myself) is a great way to introduce accountability and sobriety with my trades. People also take losses in every market by trying to time the market and guessing wrong. As I've seen with day trading crypto, trading the chops (when the coin goes up and down within a small percentage repeatedly) is a very hard thing to do correctly and it often results in losses. It's best to avoid altogether.

Other people play it correctly enough to add to their holdings. Some short calls are right in sight and "easy" to pull off with some patience if you recognize what the chart is telling you through sound Technical Analysis (TA) principles.

Learning TA principles

If you are not familiar with charts and TA, then start very small and learn through trial and error. Your best bet is to stick with us on CoinSavage.com to learn what our experts are predicting for the markets ahead.
If you would like to do some self-teaching (always recommended) there are several videos on YouTube that can help you learn some of the terminology, formations and methods of trading. Most of the important teachings are free on YouTube and you can quickly learn from simple chart descriptions and narration. A good YouTube series to look at are done by "Your Trading Coach"

https://www.youtube.com/yourtradingcoach

Your Trading Coach will teach you what chart patterns mean and how to look for them in order to know what direction the market is moving in. Learning to identify these patterns is a tool you should have to help give you an edge in investing. Another great resource for crypto trading information is:

(https://www.TechnicallyCrypto.com - Tell Larry I said hello). These are just two options among many others but they're the best that I've seen for educating new investors.

Why do you want to learn chart patterns?

These chart patterns will allow you to more reasonably predict which direction the coin is going in and how far. This will be very familiar to you if you've traded stocks before. If you do learn them well, you will be ahead of most in the crypto world. This means making more money.

While knowing chart patterns will provide you with an ability to defend your earnings, of course it's not that simple. If everyone just needed to know how to read a chart, wouldn't everyone be rich? Keep that in mind through this advice…. because no matter how well armed you are with techniques, knowledge and theory…. you can't control market outcomes.

In conclusion

Overall, despite how Lamborghini free this year has been for the majority of us, it's necessary to step back and refresh our minds a bit about the nature of what we are involved in.

Remember the underlying principles of crypto, market cycles and relax. This journey has only just begun. Since writing the first edition of these books, several changes have occurred both within the crypto market as well as externally that I'll be covering as we go forward.

We've gone through a period of extreme growth followed by several corrections and bear runs. It's important in moments like these to always remember the long-term trends and not fear the unknown. This book will help you understand this and much more in your journey into the world of crypto investing.

Thank you for your purchase; let's get to it.

-D.M. Brooks, December 2018.

Chapter 1: Crypto Background

If you are just getting started to crypto, you're in the right spot. For the next two chapters, I will be explaining crypto from the beginner mindset, and try to educate on what this technology is trying to accomplish. If you already know these basics, then you might want to skip ahead. If you're still interested in learning what has people so excited about crypto (like Bitcoin), then forge ahead.

Welcome to crypto-currency! Congratulations for taking the first step to being an early adopter in the next large technological revolution. You deserve a lot of credit for coming here before the next wave of investors and I want to help you get started.

This is the bear market version of a book that I decided to write after seeing so many headlines and articles written in the news about the performance of Bitcoin. There have been a couple of documentaries about it as well. What a lot of people right now are struggling to understand is what these coins are, what they can be used for and where this whole "crypto-currency thing" could be going.

While I don't profess to be clairvoyant and able to predict the future, I can write based on the past as well as give you an idea about what this market is doing and why you should remain interested in it.

The explosion of crypto-currency over the last three years from a small and dedicated online community into an attention-getting headline investment being espoused by A-list celebrities has been quite a transformation.

So has the silence once the euphoria stage of the market cycle ended! The wisdom imparted in this guide will help you find your way in the silent bear market and prepare best for the next cycle.

The growth of the last three years has been both spectacular in how quickly it ramped up (Bitcoin went from $5000 to $19,000 within three weeks!) as well as how quickly it crashed back down (current low pegged $3100).

This rapid movement is common in speculative investments and still catches investor's off-guard when the gains and losses are so drastic.

If at any time you run into something requiring additional explanation, feel free to write me your questions on Twitter @DM_BrooksCrypto and I'll respond back as quickly as I can.

In the meantime, let's dig in a little bit into what crypto-currency is, how it came about and more dealing with it's background.

To understand crypto-currency, one must first understand the limitations of fiat, or paper money and the centralization of it to governments and governing bodies (For example, the European Union).

Once paper money was disconnected from gold and silver, it turned into a system of money that had value based on perception more than any concrete physical items.

This is what I'm referring to when I say fiat currency; not the Italian car company.

Fiat currency is in use around the modern world, and it is a system that has the ability to increase or decrease circulation/supply of money to help control inflation or deflation.

By being controlled in a centralized fashion, governments can effectively control the wealth and the purchasing power of their citizens through the amount of money supply printed by their treasury.

This has had mostly good effects if you were to look at the growth of stock markets and GDP (Gross Domestic Product) over the last fifty years.

Since moving off of the Gold Standard (when all U.S. money was backed by its equivalent in physical gold) on August 15th, 1971 (when President Nixon announced the move to fiat currency), the U.S. market in particular rocketed from a DOW Jones of 856 up to it's current 24,688 of October 26, 2018.

That kind of growth looks and feels great to long-term investors, but it can also have bad compounding inflationary effects if there is too much paper money being printed by the treasury.

For example, the results are downright disastrous if your government isn't very stable such as what occurred in Zimbabwe during the 2000's, when the government printed currency into the trillions on paper money.

By increasing the amount of paper money in circulation, it increased inflation rates a staggering 79,600,000,000% by 2008!

This made the paper currency worthless for Zimbabwean citizens. Imagine being paid your current salary but not being able to afford a loaf of bread. (See image 1 on pg. 24 for an example of hyperinflation).

Another example of financial collapse of an economy is sadly occurring in Venezuela this year as the socialist government policies led to a complete collapse in their economy.

When this happens, citizens like us are unable to afford adequate food, water, power or anything else that we tend to take for granted. As tragic as the situation in Venezuela has become, it is not unique for a socialist economy or uncommon when a government overextends its currency and budget. (See Greece in the late 2000's).

Despite the horrors of a collapsed economy, there was a sliver of hope shown. In a first for such an economic collapse, savvy residents of Venezuela were using Bitcoin to feed their families. While the decentralized aspect has been one of the main reasons for why Bitcoin continued to succeed, here was the first real use case during a time of tragedy and despair.

The economic tragedy in Greece is another case where government monetary policies harmed the populace and significantly decreased the value of their currency.

These examples are not to say that this will happen in the United States (at least not expected to for awhile), but it does show how relying on a centralized money supply has a potential, albeit extreme, downside in cases of socialist, or a dictatorship, or Western European austerity-afflicted economies.

Side note: my friend Jeff snagged a couple hundred trillion in Zimbabwean money off eBay for $5 a few years back (As image 1 below shows). Maybe someday that'll be worth something, Jeff.

(Image 1 – Imagine buying bread with this)

That can leave us within the realm of healthy skepticism and lingering doubts about the long-term health of global economic systems at the nation-state level. As governments continue to print money with no tangible element backing their value, there's a slight risk of inflation and spending getting out of control.

However by no means is this an alarmist call to flock to crypto currency with a mindset like a Prepper.

It's just to raise awareness on how much speculation, perception and belief is built into the current fiat system rather than items of supreme stored value. As commonly as crypto is disregarded as a scam, it's helpful to compare it to what is not.

When you look at what constitutes money on a philosophical level, does the physical kind of currency matter as long as items, services or ideas of value are exchanged properly?

Look at the money in your bank account. Who or what ascribes value to it vs. material goods? The banking system and government does…but does the technology itself? Not really. We just believe that the money exists behind every dollar, or that the banks can cover all of their debts…that the government can simply create enough wealth to keep the machine rolling further into the future.

This belief and perception in fiat money is where crypto currencies are heading.

The centralization of currency, while working to most people's benefit on a macro-scale, also theoretically leads to an infinite money supply should the economy drop into a large enough recession. If your country is not run well, or the economic system is either a dictatorship, socialist or communist, there is a real risk of the money "running out". Outside of sound fiscal monetary policies and regulations set by legitimate governments, the fiat money supply would only be limited by the amount of currency that a government or body could print! As seen in Zimbabwe, Venezuela and other afflicted countries, entire economic systems with poor fiscal policy can lead to currency that becomes essentially worthless.

In more developed countries, we take stability for granted. This stability should be cherished because we are the fortunate.

Stability of our monetary system is a built-in expectation for many growing up in the developed world. As we've seen from less fortunate areas of the world, real economic tragedies can occur that can drastically alter life for people within those ravaged countries. As we've seen in Venezuela, crypto-currency is a potential solution or work around to these ills and it provided people with the purchasing power to survive when the stability in their fiat system collapsed.

Trivia Time: How many printers did Zimbabwe have in order to make their currency effectively worthless? Imagine the amount of ink used!

That's horrible what happened to those countries, but how does that explain crypto if you live in a stable country and economic system?

Before Bitcoin could be started successfully, we have to look at the American system of centralized currency with its lack of visibility into the Federal Reserve, the perception/belief in fiat value, as well as a newfound heavy skepticism that bankers and banking institutions have society's best interests in mind (stemming from the global economic collapse of 2008-2009).

These factors converged during the 2008 global economic collapse and are what provided the gasoline and matches in an environment that prompted a group of private citizens to create the crypto-currency world's first household name "Bitcoin" and ultimately the entire crypto-currency ecosystem.

Bitcoin was created by an underground group of coding "pirates" that also shared the skepticism of the banking system, the banker elite themselves, government monetary policy, and it's overreach during the global financial collapse of 2008.

This collapse was absolutely massive in reach and threatened the world order of governments across the globe itself. Bailouts to banking/private sectors and quantitative easing (QE) were the chosen methods to mitigate a true disaster.

The creativity inherent in Bitcoin was born from this fear of what the future would hold after this collapse and the skepticism that it could ever fully correct itself. QE continues to this day, for example.

How bad was the 2008 global collapse? The collapse was so big and so deep that massive taxpayer funded bailouts occurred across multiple industries in attempts just to stop the bleeding. Unemployment skyrocketed, banks had to be shut down and consolidated, new waves of regulations were passed to require banks to pass stringent "stress tests" and the housing market in the U.S. collapsed. It took several years to shake off the effects from this recession and even now, in 2018, ten years later…. there are still economic indicators left over from this event.

History books and documentaries were written and movies filmed about it. This epic failure of banks and governments across the world created an environment ripe for innovation.

This environment, with long held beliefs in the stock market, Wall Street and global monetary policy came crashing down and had a real impact on millions of people. For the first time in post-WW2 America, the economy stopped working for the middle class. Jobs and homes were lost in this economic churn. This economic attack on the American Dream led the charge for a consortium of computer code ninjas to start the work on a new system of currency.

The currency was to be decentralized with no central power dictating currency flow, built on a public ledger for transparency, and able to sent peer to peer.

This idea of decentralization, where there would be no middlemen or banks taking fees out of other people's money, is a revolution we have not seen in currency successfully before. This is a libertarian idea of no government oversight expanded into finance.

With all this said, an ideology only goes so far without results, and to date, Bitcoin and other coins have created a new class of billionaires and millionaires unlike most stock investments of the last decade. This new class of wealthy investors can be as young as 14 years old (since the only limiting factor was access to computer networks and a Google search.) This shift in wealth generation away from traditional stocks and into crypto-currencies is crucial to showcasing the potential and promise of the crypto-currency movement.

While the crypto-currency movement has grown by staggering amounts the last few years, as with most large increases in market value, there were pessimists/realists ready to decry the movement as a bubble. The negative connotation of something being a "bubble" is that it is a scam or not a long-term investment. While the rapid gain in crypto value over the last quarter of 2017 spoke to market dynamics that could not sustain themselves IE bubble, the market cycle was actually quite normal. Here's why: Imagine investing in Bitcoin in 2016 when it cost $600. Today, in October of 2018, that same investment is worth $6,400. Negative people would talk about how it went up to $19,500 and fell down to $6400 but you've 10x'd your initial investment in under two years.

If you are an alarmist or contrarian, this may

be the wrong book for you. If you truly believe that we are witnessing a technological revolution within currency, or at least the earliest stages of a new payment method then hold on because we are going to enjoy this together as the early-adopters to a transformative technology.

As a general rule in investing, it's important to note that past performance does not guarantee future performance so if at any point you are feeling uneasy or ready to pull out of the crypto-market, that is entirely your decision and at your own discretion.

While I wouldn't put all of my children's college savings into crypto-currency, I do feel relatively confident that the value will continue to increase over time and that we did not see the end of Bitcoin growth just because one market cycle ended. (Image 2).

The future value of Bitcoin is up to you to decide, but I wouldn't have written an entire book on a passing trend. Keep in mind that the same people advising against these coins back in 2011 are still there now doing the same fear mongering that costs people money in lost opportunity.

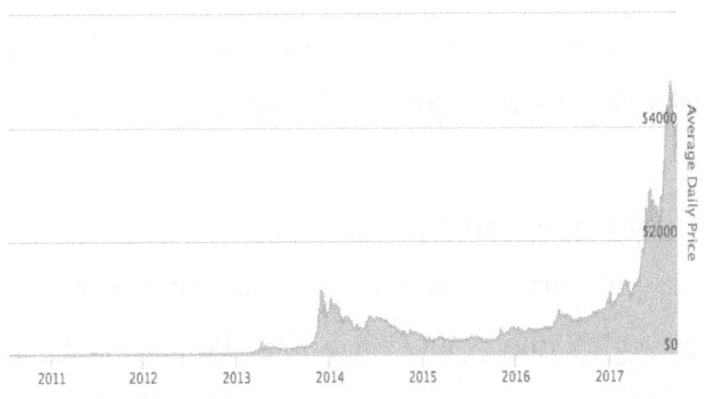

(Image 2- If you invested in Bitcoin back in 2011, you aren't reading this book)

Skepticism towards new technology is both expected and healthy; however playing it safe offers the lowest returns in investments.

While you never want to put everything you own into one basket, there's little harm in betting in crypto-currency as long as it is with money that you can afford to lose and you maintain a long-term perspective. That doesn't mean that you will automatically lose or make money, just be prepared and know that as with all speculative investments, there is volatility that carries inherent risk.

Another way to think about investing in crypto-currency is as the natural progression of technology. Way back in the beginning in time, products were bartered with rocks, stones, rare minerals, materials, gold and silver. As the world grew and countries were formed, wars started to be fought over these natural resources since they could not be easily duplicated.

Imagine fighting a world war for the paper money in your pocket today like had be done with gold for centuries.

Another drawback to these older monetary assets was the ability to carry or transport these minerals. Aside from ships or horseback, large transfers of funds were difficult to accomplish. (Imagine buying a home or vehicle in rocks).

Once the printing press was invented, countries began to print their own specific money that could be used within their borders, regions or across nations. The advent of paper money was incredible! Amounts of gold, silver and other trinkets of value could be linked to a simple piece of paper that could be easily transported. Paper money could also be destroyed and relatively easily replaced, unlike a chunk of gold or silver.

This system of paper money lasted for centuries and it was not until the age of the Internet where the next major shift began in money: the use of data to transfer money online.

Much like how the Internet turned brick and mortar stores into eBay shops, cryptocurrency aims to turn these pieces of paper money in your wallet or bank into a digital coin, which can be used for all transactions using the increasingly globally connected Internet.

This technological evolution can be seen in other mediums. For example, newspapers and magazines slowly led to websites. Bitcoin and crypto turn cash (newspapers, brick and mortar shops) into eBay, Amazon, or digital financial value (Bitcoin).

When we refer to crypto-currency think of it as a new world of technology just starting to form itself. The next chapter will explain this further.

Chapter 2: What is Crypto-Currency?

As discussed, Crypto-Currency is a digital asset that can be used for transactions, and acts just like traditional currency except it is entirely digital and online. There are no actual coins or paper money associated with crypto-currency. It's essentially 1's and 0's in thin air, delivered through computer networks and showing up in your trading or bank account. Imagine ordering this book off of Amazon and instead of using your credit card or PayPal, you would instead send me a digital coin.

Rather than using your credit card number, you would put in the amount you wish to send and then type in the unique address of the person that is receiving the payment, and by clicking send the transaction is then on its way.

Same concept and method to use Amazon, the only change is the payment source and its routing. Crypto-currency acts like any other kind of currency but with several key differences, advantages and disadvantages:

The very first difference is that Bitcoin (for example) can be decentralized. No government, no controlling entity, no sanctioning body, no company, nor any one person controls it. In order to make a system or network change, Bitcoin developers and miners (more on this in a bit) need to come to an agreement. These are not common or easy to do since developers and miners are by the very nature of crypto- across the globe and decentralized.

When they do manage to agree, a "hard fork" occurs where the original coin code continues to exist but then an offshoot of that code is created for people to use instead.

That occurred in August 2017 when Bitcoin Cash was created from a hard fork in Bitcoin code by some of the community desiring a code change to make Bitcoin more capable of handling larger transactions. (Side Note: This fork created a lot of drama within the Bitcoin community that persists to this day due to the personalities involved.)

Crypto-currency can also be limited in production. For example, Bitcoin (the most popular of all crypto-coins based on market cap as of this writing) is limited to 21 million coins.

Litecoin, another crypto-coin, is limited to 84 million coins. Meanwhile, Ethereum (yet another coin—just wait) has no limits to its amount of coins. This has a slight impact on coin value in theory. Powerful computer farms, instead of using printers to print more paper money, can "mine" crypto-currency.

Coins can be mined? What is mining?
Mining is the term for what happens when the distributed network of computers that are crunching the advanced calculations required to write to the public ledger for a coin get rewarded for this effort.
The reward is the creation of more coins. When someone is a Bitcoin (or any coin) miner, that is what they are doing: running computers that solve advanced calculations required to write to the public ledger of a coin and being rewarded for it with coins of their own.

Some coins require more processing power than others to mine profitably, but it's safe to say that for the vast majority of current coins, the computers required are beyond consumer grade laptops or desktops.

The average consumer mining setup starts around $300 and can go up from there. While it's nice to dream of building a mining "rig" to make money in the background while you go about your daily routine, it's important to know that due to electricity costs in the U.S., mining is very difficult to do profitably. Because of the electrical costs, very few of us will make money mining ourselves. It costs money to make less money!

The coins created through mining are essentially digital signatures that have been completed through advanced mathematical calculations done by these racks of powerful computers. The mining software may change, as does the method of the calculations (which helps drive the computer processing power requirements).

This is where someone in mining should check out the 2nd Edition where I get into more of the economics around mining and what it may take.

Moving on to coin creation. With a "coin" created, the next thing you're going to want to do is to use it for a transaction or store it.

How are transactions different with crypto-coins? Well, first transactions are publicly recorded in the blockchain ledger. This statement carries a lot of information that I will break down and simplify for you. **Blockchain is the underlying technology behind the entire crypto-currency technology.** To quote and paraphrase Wikipedia, "Blockchain is a distributed database that is used to maintain a continuously growing list of records, called blocks. Each block contains a timestamp and a link to a previous block. A blockchain is resistant to modification of data by design, once a block is recorded, it cannot be altered retroactively without the alteration of all subsequent blocks and a collusion of the network majority." (IE: miners) What does this mean for crypto-currency? Simply that the ledger for all transactions conducted is public, recorded, able to be verified, won't allow for double payments, and is essentially permanent in recording these transactions which prevents fraudulent changes to transactions later (cooking the books, double counting, etc.)

Blockchain is extremely important because it facilitates the ability for a decentralized currency. With no centralized overhead controlling ledgers, the blockchain can operate openly and without potential for fraudulent bookkeeping or double counting of transactions.

The amount of technology in the blockchain and crypto-currency in general is rapidly advancing and changing seemingly every month. Large banks are now using blockchain technology themselves in order to make their operations more efficient. Sounds like an endorsement of the technology to me.

As an investor, it is important to stay informed by visiting crypto-news sites, twitter accounts, and sometimes Reddit in order to stay informed. Since all of crypto-currency is based on digital assets tied to blockchain technology, you will need to gain a sense of digital knowledge about them and their specific functions and features. What are the problems the coin is attempting to solve?

That's not to say that you will need to know every byte that goes into each coin, but some idea of the development roadmap for each coin is a better way to figure out the potential market value of your investment. Find out who is working on the teams for each coin you're investing in. A strong management team lends itself to a positive future outlook. It will also guide you with selecting which feature sets of different coins are more likely to succeed.

Another point to bring up is that while these technologies are improving and expanding through adoption, what becomes mainstream later may not look anything like what we are seeing right now.

Take Ethereum for example:

This is a powerful blockchain application technology, not truly a currency, that may result in great changes in financial banking or it could help power Artificial Intelligence (AI) in the future. It's still very early, so the investment bet with Ethereum is on potential and promise of the blockchain application technology more than it being a currency. Think of Ethereum in some ways as an operating system like what is found on your phone or laptop. Using that operating system, a lot of things can be built.

We've learned several key items about what crypto-currency consists of in this section, but this has been a high level overview. If you would like to learn more, I highly suggest reading crypto-specific news sites and blogs. I'll mention a few in the additional resources section at the end of this book to help you get started.

When doing your research, it's important to make sure that you are getting information from a reputable source that is not tied directly to anyone that is invested in a particular coin. During the 2017 frenzy, there were a lot of fraudulent coins developed for elaborate pump and dump schemes. Quite a few of these even used plagiarized white papers to explain their technology! Imagine copy pasting from a legitimate crypto development white paper and then making millions off of it.

The goal from doing that was generate enough interest in the fraudulent or non-existent crypto-coin through the use of marketing.

After the interest is achieved, an ICO (or initial coin offering) would be scheduled for people to buy in, much like an IPO (initial public offering) on the stock market.
Not all coins or ICOs are equal and the SEC (Securities and Exchange Commission), as well as China are investigating and in China's case, outright banning the practice of ICOs due to the amount of scams that have occurred with fake coins.

This is the kind of scenario that makes a lot of casual investors lose money or decide against investing altogether in this market. It needs to end.

The caveat emptor saying must ring in everyone's head when looking into smaller alternate coins. As the market matures, more and more of these coins will go belly up. Thankfully, with the bear market of 2018, a lot of them effectively have. Expect this trend to continue as the market continues to mature through use cases of different applications of crypto-currency and blockchain.

As you invest in coins, always ask yourself, "What problem is the coin trying to solve?" Who are the developers? Does this feel like a pump and dump scheme ICO that is intended to only make the founders rich? How many well-known people are investing in it? What is the market cap and expected price?

ICOs and smaller coins will require you to do your research, but do not be afraid.

Much like the Internet of the 1990's, some companies (or coins) will be scams and some will be the next Amazon, eBay, Alibaba, etc. It is very important to recognize that since the market is still so new, there will be a bit of a Wild West factor to it but the volatility drives returns higher than blue chip stocks will.

You will only be 100% safe if you stick with the proven coins and avoid ICOs.
By sticking with the coins that have the largest market caps, you are going to be a safer investor that will not have to worry about scammers and ICOs. At least not until more controls are put in place to protect investors.

This is one of the risks of being an early adopter in any technology. If it were not crypto coins, it would be something or someone else looking to take advantage of new investors to any deregulated market.

The good news to this technology is that all transactions are recorded publically and there's no reasonable ability to go back and change an entry, so it's going to be harder and harder to launder money, if not impossible. Think of the ways this would benefit our banking systems, financial reporting, stock markets and company quarterly reports if nothing could be hidden related to finances and transactions.

Hopefully this helps to paint a picture of what crypto-currency is and why it's received so much attention from early adopters and investors. The benefits it can bring to society are immense.

At the bare minimum, it promises more accuracy in recording of transactions, a huge reduction in potential fraud, the end of double counting and a system that is nearly impossible to take over and attack.

Thousands or millions of computers all separated track each transaction – good luck trying to hack every one of them in order to change the blockchain.

Now that you understand some of the technology behind crypto-currency, you may want to know how it can be used in your daily life. The answer is both simple and nuanced which we will get into in the next chapter.

Chapter 3: How Is Crypto-Currency Used?

Before I describe how it can be used, you are going to need to know the advantages, disadvantages of using crypto-currency.

What are the advantages to crypto-currency? Well, with the currency based on a blockchain, the ledger is public and highly secure due to the distributed nature of the database that it is on. This means that double transactions are no longer possible and no central authority is needed to oversee transactions since they are secured (and unable to be reasonably altered).

With the advantage of a highly secure distributed network that publically records transactions and makes double spending impossible, crypto-currency also has the advantage of not being limited by the economic conditions of the state or country that its users are in.

This means that artificial inflation and a Zimbabwe or Venezuelan disaster is minimized through the inability to just print more money. This is especially important when discussing Bitcoin or other currencies with a set maximum amount of coins. As supply of the coins runs out, the currency will actually have a <u>deflationary</u> effect.

The deflationary aspect of Bitcoin is when the limited number of coins available means value will continue to increase along with its purchasing power.

This is unlike the US Dollar, where printing more money only lessens the purchasing power of one dollar.

Another advantage is that since everything is online, the borders of the user's country do not limit the use of crypto-currency. A buyer in Japan can transact with a seller in the UK without having to pay conversion fees or lose value since crypto isn't tied to any single county's monetary system. In other words, one Bitcoin is worth one Bitcoin everywhere on the planet.

Another way it can be used is as an investment, which is why you're reading this book. As an investment, it is important to realize that the largest gains with any new technology occur the earlier you invest in the market.

As Geoffrey Moore has written extensively about, there are stages to any new technology.

It's important that you learn about these stages and how they will impact the upcoming revolution of crypto-currency. (See Image 3)

To highlight the stages of crypto-currency investing, we are no longer in the innovator period.

Instead we are now inching through the early adopter mode, which is a great place to be as an investor because it's before the Early Majority/mainstream gets involved (institutional banks, investors with large holdings, mom and dad, etc.). Here is a visual overview of how the progression of new technology occurs:

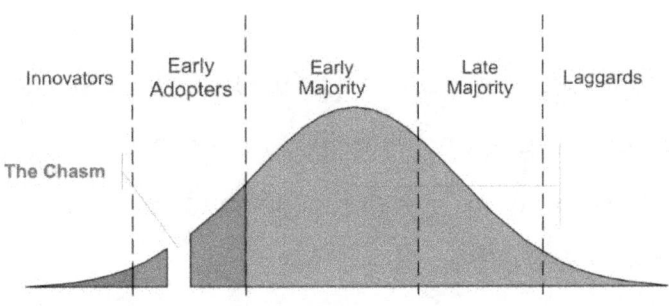

(Image 3 – The technology adoption curve)

The innovators are the people who developed and bought into Bitcoin before 2014. They are now the millionaires and billionaires helping to shape the future of crypto-currency or enjoying life on their yacht. Maybe both. What you will find after them are the early adopters like us that see the potential for a massive wave of change. As of late 2018, we are going to be transitioning over the next year or two into the Early Majority period as large banking institutions, well-known investors and vast sums of money begins to get involved in Bitcoin. The wheels of progress haven't stopped despite the bear market.

What all of this means is quite clear: If Jaime Dimon is right, and Bitcoin is a "fraud that will just blow up", then it's going to blow up the largest institutions with it.

(Side Note: While speaking about Bitcoin as a fraud, JP Morgan Securities was caught buying Bitcoin in large chunks on foreign exchanges. Yet another advantage of having a public ledger.)

Now with the basic advantages out of the way, its important to note the disadvantages of crypto-currency.

For the first disadvantage, crypto-currency is only online. There are no physical coins that have value off of the Internet. What this means is that unless the transaction is capable to be completed online where crypto-currency is accepted, you won't be able to use it without converting it back to fiat in your home country. If your power grid goes down, you might have some problems. However, if that were to happen today…the same problems would tend to exist.

This accessibility to the crypto-coins in everyday life is slowly changing for the better, but it will be a few years before your local Target or Wal-Mart will accept them.

However, with that said, there are rumors that Amazon will be accepting Bitcoin soon and Overstock.com has accepted crypto-currency now!

The tide is changing, and once we get into the Early Majority phase you will start to see the familiar "Bitcoin accepted here" logo at most cash registers.

Another disadvantage of crypto-currency is that we simply cannot predict accurately where their value is going to be 5-10 years from now.

We can forecast and project, but no one truly knows how much one Bitcoin will be worth in 2025. If they say that they do, don't use them for investment advice.

Finally, the other main disadvantage that you need to be aware of is that cyber attacks do happen and people have lost their coins through them. As a matter of being an online citizen of the Internet, you must practice a smart approach to cyber security. To borrow from the movie Fight Club, the very first rule of investing in crypto-currency is to not talk about investing in crypto-currency. The less people know about your investments, the smaller of a target you become. Treat this like you would treat the amount of cash you have in the bank. No need to advertise it. There are other ways to protect your investments of course. The ultimate defense against losing your hard-earned coin stash is to buy a hardware wallet for them. Out of the hardware wallets available, I recommend the Ledger Nano S to store your coins offline safely.

Good security practices are a must if you start to invest beyond a casual amount that you're ok with losing. With that said, as long as you aren't leaving thousands (or millions) of dollars on open exchanges, sharing the amount you have invested, publically list your email address and go on Reddit to tell people: you'll more than likely be ok. If you do decide to do those things, then you're an idiot.

As we discussed in the advantages section, crypto-currency (mainly Bitcoin) can be used to conduct transactions online with a few online vendors as well as make payments in some foreign countries and some local shops where Bitcoin is accepted. This acceptance is expected to grow internationally and signs of gradual acceptance are becoming more frequent.

There are now Bitcoin ATMs popping up around the US and Europe too, for those of you so inclined. These allow you to buy and sometimes sell Bitcoin for cash. The crypto payment method is slowly growing in popularity and acceptance so that within a decade, it is safe to expect it to be used to order nearly everything you could possibly want online or in person. Bitcoin acceptance is now appearing on several online store websites lately too.

So how can crypto-currency be used? Many different ways, much like any legal tender. However as hinted about above, there is one more usage for it that is going to be a large advantage internationally:

It can be used as a safe harbor of stored value for when fiat based economies struggle or go into recessions.

Since crypto-currency is completely separate from fiat, it does not possess direct ties to the fortunes of the global stock markets. Instead, it could act as a place to store money while the traditional markets retract during the cyclical recessions that occur. Since Bitcoin has not existed during a true recession before, watching the global markets in 2019-2020 will be crucial to understanding proper entry points for buying into crypto.

A shrewd investor would simply move their assets around during this time to help protect their wealth. In theory, this could lead to even greater gains to investors of crypto-currency that had held on from before the recession took place. It remains to be seen if this theory holds water, but as explained above – it could depend on the severity of a global recession.

Typically, during those periods of recession, speculatory investments such as Bitcoin and crypto tend to lose liquidity as buyers look to protect their money. Bitcoin may trend differently in such a scenario only due to its use as a currency itself, not directly tied to the health of a government's currency. (Meaning 1 Bitcoin costs 1 Bitcoin regardless of USD value)

Aside from the retail aspects of crypto, the investment choice is clear and of the most importance right now. As an investor eager to make money, crypto-currency's best use right now is as a store of value. That store of value is currently under attack with a declining market, so as we speak right now, it's in theory.

You invest your fiat into it and wait for it to gain acceptance, go mainstream and have large investors come into the market in order to raise its value.

If you are so inclined to trade with it, you can ride the waves of appreciation and depreciation to make some returns as well. Heck, you can even day trade crypto-currency just like stocks with some trading platforms. (Want to short a coin? You can!)

Several people do this and have made a lot of money just by applying some old fashioned Technical Analysis to different coins. While not as stable as the NASDAQ, it was vastly rewarding to those that timed their trades correctly.

Hopefully, this basic rundown provides you with a backdrop of the highlights of cryptocurrency. You now understand the basic theory of the blockchain, what cryptocurrency can and cannot do, as well as what it's advantages and disadvantages are at this current time.

I'd only like to add one more thought before ending this chapter:

Reading this book in 2018 gets you ahead of the learning curve for many future investors and your knowledge of the crypto market will grow as the market cycles continue.

Despite this bear market, it has still been a steady climb from the days when you could buy or mine thousands of Bitcoin for next to nothing.

The value has only continued to increase gradually as the technology has matured and grown. For this reason, among the others listed, you will make money as an early adopter if you are patient, avoid jumping in while the market is still bottoming out (unless you have long-term patience) and make sound investment decisions in the right coins.

When this bear market runs out, large gains from buying in at super low entry prices will come with a cost. That cost? Taxes. It's important that you follow the tax laws of your country. For the next section, we will cover what the IRS (Internal Revenue Service) says about crypto-currency. Thankfully for us, the IRS made crypto investing much clearer in the U.S. with the Tax Law of 2018.

Chapter 4: Taxes and Crypto

In How Anyone Can Invest 2nd Edition, we covered the tax implications of investing in crypto-currency under the old tax guidance rules from the IRS that were published in 2014. The new Tax Law of 2018 continues these definitions but ended the "like-kind" loophole, which some crypto investors were incorrectly using to take profits from one coin into another without paying taxes on it.

I'm a big fan of the changes in the 2018 Tax Law concerning this because not only was "like-kind" usage in crypto total BS, but it also makes reporting of crypto gains and losses much simpler for everyone by keeping things cut and dry simple.

I'm assuming that people know that you are taxed on investment gains in the U.S. and must pay the IRS the taxes required from it.

It wasn't until I was asked directly about if I paid taxes on my own gains that I realized that people are not sure where Bitcoin or crypto-coins fit within the tax codes.

As amazing as crypto-currency is, as decentralized as it may be, you have to pay taxes on any income you've gotten from it. **I would never tell anyone to not pay taxes on their crypto-investments.** While this section is best left to your CPA, what I can do is help guide you a little on what to do and how to prepare for taxes with your crypto-investments.

Note that I am not a CPA (Certified Public Accountant), nor am pretending to be one. I would recommend that you hire a CPA that is familiar with the tax codes around crypto-currency if you have trouble with TurboTax.

This section is written for the U.S. only, if you live elsewhere please research your own tax laws and consult with a professional.

Ok, with that out of the way, the very first thing to know is that the IRS defines crypto-currencies as PROPERTY.

What this means is that you must pay taxes on capital gains or losses every time you dispose of the crypto-currency. For example, a purchase of 1 Bitcoin for $2900, then a sale of that same 1 Bitcoin a few months later for $3800, will now owe tax on the $900 profit.

Another thing to keep in mind with crypto-currency being labeled as property is that it is included in your annual income. For example, Kyle makes $70,000 a year gross from his job.

If he buys and sells Bitcoin like the example above, then his total taxable gross income is now $70,900 for the year.

This can have major implications for your taxes if you have invested a lot of money, bought a lot of coins, then sold them and made a lot of money. This scenario could have the effect of moving you up into a higher tax bracket where your total income is taxed at a higher rate!

In using Bitcoin as the example, I am not stating that the other coins avoid taxes. Instead, I am just using the most widely used and invested crypto-currency for the example. When you consult with a CPA, I'd recommend using the Bitcoin name to start your discussions about crypto-currency investments to judge how in-depth their knowledge is of these investments.

From there you can discuss how you own $xyz of coins in XMR, DASH, Monero, XRP, etc. (these are alternative crypto-coins commonly available)

What else should you know about taxes with crypto-currency investing?

Unlike with cash, when you spend crypto currency, it is really two transactions in one: disposing of the crypto-currency and then spending the cash-equivalent amount (1 Bitcoin sold off at $3800 and taxed, then spending $3800 on an item, which may be taxed).

Business transactions in crypto-currencies are subject to all the normal rules for sales tax, withholding, and information reporting, which means that just like your other business transactions you will need to keep detailed records of every transaction in crypto-currencies so that your income is accurately measured.

Now let's investigate what the IRS classifies crypto-currency as, because this is important for understanding how to arrange your investments at tax time.

First, the IRS refers to Bitcoin and crypto-currency as "Virtual Currency". This is important when reading through the tax terms used by them in allocating Bitcoin as property.

As we've discussed, for federal tax purposes, crypto-currency is treated as property. General tax principles that apply to transactions of property apply to transactions using crypto-currency.

Some tidbits to know for taxes include:

- "A taxpayer who receives virtual currency as payment for goods or services must, in computing gross income, include the fair market value of the virtual currency, measured in U.S. dollars, as of the date that the virtual currency was received."
- "Virtual currency that has an equivalent value in real currency, or

that acts as a substitute for real currency, is referred to as "convertible" virtual currency. Bitcoin is one example of a convertible virtual currency. Bitcoin can be digitally traded between users and can be purchased for, or exchanged into, U.S. dollars, Euros, and other real or virtual currencies."
- "Transactions using virtual currency must be reported in U.S. dollars" on the tax return.
- "Taxpayers will be required to determine the fair market value of virtual currency in U.S. dollars as of the date of payment or receipt."
- "If a virtual currency is listed on an exchange and the exchange rate is established by market supply and demand, the fair market value of the virtual currency is determined by converting the virtual currency into U.S. dollars ... at the exchange rate, in a reasonable manner that is consistently applied."

The IRS also answers a couple relevant questions on their website, so I recommend you go and read through it, as well as provide it to your CPA at tax time. Some of these questions and answers are as follows:

Q–6: Does a taxpayer have gain or loss upon an exchange of virtual currency for other property?

A–6: Yes. If the fair market value of property received in exchange for virtual currency exceeds the taxpayer's adjusted basis of the virtual currency, the taxpayer has taxable gain. The taxpayer has a loss if the fair market value of the property received is less than the adjusted basis of the virtual currency.

Q–8: Does a taxpayer who "mines" virtual currency (for example, uses computer resources to validate Bitcoin transactions and maintain the public Bitcoin transaction ledger) realize gross income upon receipt of the virtual currency resulting from those activities?

A–8: Yes, when a taxpayer successfully "mines" virtual currency, the fair market value of the virtual currency as of the date of receipt is includible in gross income.

Q–12: Is a payment made using virtual currency subject to information reporting?

A–12: A payment made using virtual currency is subject to information reporting to the same extent as any other payment made in property. For example, a person who in the course of a trade or business makes a payment of fixed and determinable income using virtual currency with a value of $600 or more to a U.S. non-exempt recipient in a taxable year is required to report the payment to the IRS and to the payee. Examples of payments of fixed and determinable income include rent, salaries, wages, premiums, annuities, and compensation.

In summary, what all of this means is that you must know these two basic tenants of crypto-currency at tax time (courtesy of Turbo Tax):

Bitcoins held as capital assets are taxed as property

If you hold crypto-currency as a capital asset, you must treat them as property for tax purposes. General tax principles applicable to property transactions apply to crypto-currency.

If your crypto-currency is held as a capital asset, like stocks or bonds, any gain or loss from the sale or exchange of the asset is taxed as a capital gain or loss. Otherwise, you will realize ordinary gain or loss on an exchange.

Crypto-Currency miners must report receipt of the crypto- currency as income

Some people "mine" Bitcoins, Litecoins, Ethereum, etc. by using computer resources to validate transactions and maintain the transaction ledger.

According to the IRS, when a taxpayer successfully "mines" crypto-currency coins and has earnings from that activity whether in the form of coins or any other form, he or she must include it in his gross income after determining the fair market dollar value of the virtual currency as of the day it was received. If a miner is self-employed, his or her gross earnings minus allowable tax deductions are also subject to the self-employment tax.

Make sure that you keep records of your transactions. Coinbase, Binance, Poloniex, Bittrex, GDAX and other sites can tabulate these for you so that you have a record at tax time. It is extremely important to have the records which will allow you to calculate your short term capital gains vs. your long term gains due to the difference in tax rate/penalty for each as you continue to invest. Don't make the mistake of getting slammed with short-term capital gains taxes when you buy and sell coins for profit. Make sure to always calculate in the tax penalties when you conduct transactions on the crypto-market in order to effectively shield yourself from an unexpectedly high tax bill.

This section contains the best starting information on this topic that you could have as it comes directly from the IRS and TurboTax. It is not a substitute for consulting with a reputable CPA and at no point in time should you solely use what is contained here when doing your year-end taxes unless you are a professional accountant and understand tax code laws.

For the casual investor, this sounds a lot more complicated than it really is and if you have ever invested in stocks, you will see similarities to investing in crypto-currencies. As technical and scary as taxes can be, just remember that this is what every investor has to go through and that even the best growth potential is taxed.

Before the IRS rules were published, there were people not paying taxes on these gains from crypto-currency. This is illegal and not something you should do unless you plan to escape the federal government and be on the run for the rest of your life. The IRS has been gearing up to proceed with tax evasion investigations since 2014 and are more prepared than ever to go after you and your property for failing to disclose gains made in crypto-currency. As of this writing, there have been exchanges contacted by the IRS with the intent of them providing access to user accounts to the IRS for investigative purposes of tax evasion. Make sure you pay your taxes!

Questions or comments? Please send a message to me on twitter at @DM_BrooksCrypto or contact a CPA professional that deals in crypto-currency for their expert opinion. As always, look at the IRS guidance and look at the basics on TurboTax's website for additional details. I will not do your taxes for you, but many others will!

Now that you've paid your taxes, let's look into trading the coins to earn gains that make the taxes that the IRS wants so interesting.

Chapter 5: Crypto Trading Strategies:

It's important to say right up front that any advice given in this section is not professional, is entirely your decision to follow and any gains or losses are solely your own and no responsibility lies with me. (Although if you make a huge profit, I will gladly accept donations!)

Before delving entirely into this topic, let's pull back and take a macro view of cryptocurrency on a few factors. The first factor that needs to be said is that we are in the middle of a gruesome Bear market that has removed almost $500 billion from the total market cap of the entire crypto market.

To put this into perspective, on December 17th, 2017 the entire crypto market cap was over $590 billion.

Almost exactly one year later (December 16th, 2018) the total market cap for crypto is $103 billion (according to CoinMarketCap).

The losses are staggering and have caused a lot of people to leave crypto investing altogether.

In fact, you can view the popularity of Bitcoin and crypto by doing a simple Google Trends search on those keywords to see just how unpopular it has become in 2018. Much like the price of Bitcoin, the searches have dropped like a rock!

This is expected to continue into 2019, but this presents us with a lot of great opportunities. I wrote an article about this on Coin Savage, which I'll share below:

After trading sideways since late summer/fall, BTC made its long awaited move. Unfortunately, it did not move where we were hoping. When an asset trades sideways, it indicates a big move coming. This led many who had been beat up during 2018 to hope for positive movement.

Positive thinking can only get us so far.

A lot of great news has come out this year to support the growing infrastructure of crypto currency. It has not resulted in the price movements that we grew to expect coming out of 2017's Bull market.

In fact, the crypto market has never looked this promising from a technological adoption perspective. Go back to 2017 and the crypto market didn't even have custody arrangements secured yet.

As you know, custody is one of the most important things for large financial firms. Custody of the asset allows these firms to create asset class holdings for their clients governed by financial regulations.

Focus on the use case

2018 will be remembered as a great year for crypto currency due to the large gains in infrastructure, regulations and the beginning of stability. It's a watershed year of necessary measures if crypto is ever going to be mainstream.

The underlying message this year that a lot of crypto may be forgetting is there needs to be a compelling use case established for Main Street as well as Wall Street. Not just promises, theories and Early Adopter tech-geek level interest.

The question we all need to answer is simply, "what will the killer application of this technology end up looking like in order for crypto to become widely used?"

Speculation vs. Real Growth

Speculatory markets are fun, volatile ways to make a lot of money in very short time periods. For most investors, they view these investments as gambling.

As we get through 2018 and look at 2019, we will need to start seeing the foundational changes begin to deliver results. If we continue to see large firms testing out different solutions, it's a good sign. If we continue to see them loosely implement them or not roll them out to the public, it'll be another long year.

My money is on 2019 leaning towards wider adoption but mixed results as we continue to see the market mature.

2018 Short Term Outlook

My personal expectation is that BTC drops further and 2019 will be a continuation of the decline we saw this year.

There will be short term trades available to take advantage of, but I think we will see the overall market cap continue to decline as the market forces go to work.

These market forces should hopefully eliminate bad ICOs, weak alt coins and projects that haven't delivered. In order for the crypto market to return, there will need to be some thinning of the herd as victors are chosen.

2018 has already done some of this painful work, but more will be needed.

Doom and Gloom?

Not at all. This is simply a sober look of low expectations for the market going forward. The technology is very real and will solve problems. It is the future. We will just have to set our expectations realistically.
Dollar Cost Averaging for the long term, close stops set for short term trading.

We are able to get excellent entry points in down markets. Accumulate your holdings and sit tight.

What is happening to Bitcoin?

If you have been into crypto for a while, you have heard variations of this question. The urgency behind this question has grown as we continue to explore the depths of the Bitcoin market bottom. We can look at charts, examine investor sentiment, watch the news, interview thought leaders in the space and come to the same conclusion: No one *really* knows. *
(* - With the exception of Mr. McAfee)

An Expert Told Me This was the Bottom!

It's very easy to grow cynical when market cycles dismiss winners from the previous bull cycle and reality starts to set in.

This reality should serve as a guide: No one can call bottom with accuracy worth putting your money on. If you follow someone who tells you that they have the formula or method that can predict the outcome as a sure thing? Run, don't walk away.

What you can do instead is listen to proven experts that have made their money in similar market cycles to understand the market trend.

The Bitcoin Market Cycle: Now what?

A lot of time has been spent exploring different trend lines and market signals. As I write this, the charts are mixed or looking downward. Does this mean it can change an hour after I submit this article?

Absolutely. Can we predict that being the end of the bear market? Highly doubtful. Herein lies what we all love and hate about crypto - it's a volatile market with very severe swings at unexpected times.

Not a Bear market cop-out

With the caveats out of the way, here are my personal thoughts on the crypto market as of December 16th, 2018 at 2:28pm EST:

- Bitcoin is the most important indicator for the health of the crypto market
- Bitcoin is not at it's bottom yet when you look at trading volumes and market buys
- If a global recession hits before the market turns around, crypto has a real risk of being severely depressed.

- We will see a lot more projects getting scrapped over the next year, which will strengthen the overall market.

No one knows what alt coins will survive but the safe money is on the majors (XRP, ETH) Dollar Cost Averaging is your friend during these cycles.

Decide if you should deploy it over the coming weeks and months.

This is not financial advice and I am not your financial advisor.

What are you doing?

My strategy has been relatively simple: I cashed out back at $6600 and have made some small trades on alt coins for minimal gains.

My plan is to back the truck up once Bitcoin gets into the $2,300-$2,700 range. (If this happens, otherwise, I'm just Dollar Cost Averaging this entire time)

That isn't necessarily the bottom but unless a global recession hits (and if it does my strategy will change), this should be a safe entry for the next market cycle.

You can also follow me by signing up to my Trade Alerts on Coin Savage.com.

Those will tell you when I buy/sell an asset and also my reasoning for doing so. (I am not your financial advisor)

Hold on tight and wait for the right entry point. The best strategy is making fewer trades and having patience right now.

We might be going lower and managing your emotional state by making and sticking with a plan will allow you to win the next Bull cycle.

This bear market can break you if you can't keep perspective. To keep perspective, it is important to continually pull back the lens and look at this from the perspective of 1994 Internet. Bitcoin has only been around since 2009 and has seen rapid growth over the previous 3 years. Prior to then, the momentum was steady, but it was slow.

All crypto-coins have taken awhile to gain value, with a few explosions; the general trend is a slow climb up over years.

This slow climb is where I base my projections and why I'm not going to tell you what you should do since every situation is personal.

What I can impart is that if you believe in blockchain technology and believe in decentralized money that is digital in nature and has the advantages that crypto-currency can bring to the table, you will find a compelling reason to invest with a long term strategy and view.

Remember – This is the natural technological progression from rocks, minerals to paper to digital. It's coming regardless of what people say, the only question is who will be there early enough to make large profits from it. If you've picked up this book and followed along with me so far, then you are an early adopter who will make money in the crypto-currency markets.

If you prefer to make money quicker, then crypto has ample opportunities available with the hundreds of smaller coins out there to turn double-digit jumps and allow people to short the market for rapid turnarounds in profits and losses.

This short term gain is not the purpose of this book, but plenty of money can be made doing it provided you know what you are doing and can accept an extremely high level of risk.

For short-term gains and action, I recommend following the principles of Technical Analysis to be sure you aren't selling at the bottom or buying at the top.

The biggest mistake I have seen people make in stocks and now crypto-coins is doing exactly this. They emotionally feel like they're missing out and get involved near the top of a cycle. Then when the market corrects, they're stuck with a loss (sometimes quite large) and are afraid of losing everything, so they sell.

What we saw in Bitcoin was prices approaching $5,000 and people deciding to go all-in (sometimes with money they couldn't afford to lose), then when it dropped down to $2900, they cashed out based off of fear, unknown and doubt (FUD). When trading anything dealing in markets, you must always maintain your sobriety and never let emotions get in the way of a good trade.

People also take losses in every market by trying to time the market and guessing wrong. As I've seen with day trading crypto, trading the chops (when the coin goes up and down within a small percentage repeatedly) is a very hard thing to do correctly and it often results in losses.

Other people play it correctly and patiently enough to add to their holdings. They will see the charts showing a small run up, but look at a variety of factors to know at what price they should sell. The price then decreases from where they had bought in at, so with the extra money, they reinvest and now hold more coins than before! This is the ideal day-trading scenario. Unfortunately, when the bear market is ongoing, it becomes much harder to predict since investors are all unsure of when it will end and how high prices can actually go in a market downtrend.

Some short calls are right in sight and easy to pull off with some patience if you recognize what the chart is telling you through sound Technical Analysis (TA) principals. Others will be misleading and cause you to lose money. The key is to win bigger than you lose. For example, you could lose $5 on every trade you make (say you've made 100) except the one trade where you made $10,000. Are you a winning trader? Most should say yes. I'm not saying go out there and lose 99 out of 100 trades, but just an extreme example to show how to approach trading from a numbers perspective.

If you are familiar with charts, I've included some patterns on the next page to get a sense of what is about to happen, based on the chart patterns.

Reversal Patterns

Double Top — stop, neckline, entry, target

Head and Shoulders — stop, neckline, entry, target

Rising Wedge — stop, entry, target

Double Bottom — target, neckline, entry, stop

Inverse Head and Shoulders — target, neckline, entry, stop

Falling Wedge — target, entry, stop

Continuation Patterns

Falling Wedge — target, entry, stop

Bullish Rectangle — target, entry, stop

Bullish Pennant — target, entry, stop

Rising Wedge — stop, entry, target

Bearish Rectangle — stop, entry, target

Bearish Pennant — stop, entry, target

Bilateral Patterns

Ascending Triangle — target, entry, entry, target

Descending Triangle — target, entry, entry, target

Symmetrical Triangle — target, entry, entry, target

It's important to note that we have seen extreme changes within the crypto-coins value in under a month. Since the crypto-markets are open 24 hours a day, seven days a week worldwide, you can see rapid price fluctuations. Think about it this way: You have over twice as many working hours in crypto-trading as you do trying to trade the regular stock market in each day with less capital moving around. Small blips in a huge stock price are equivalent to large moves in a much smaller crypto market. This means that when short term trading, you can't make guesses on developing patterns within a short window like 15 minutes. It means next to nothing most of the time. You'll want to pull back your view to 60 minutes, the 4-hour, the daily and even the weekly view to help guide you in terms of where the market or coin could be heading. With so many people involved across the world, it makes it hard to accurately predict more than 4 hours ahead, and that is reserved to the people who know what they're looking at after years of trading. This is all said not to dissuade you from day trading crypto, but more to serve as a guide for what to look out for and what to keep in mind before you set your limits and start shorting coins. I don't recommend this for beginners to investing. If you've done this before with stocks, you'll really enjoy the rush that crypto trading can bring.

What chart patterns are showing you are ways to look at each coin and attempt to predict which direction the coin is going in. These are going to be very familiar to you if you've traded stocks before.

Overall, I'm not sure you can go entirely wrong either way you play it (short term or long term), but based on the historical gains and technological momentum, my own money is on a mix of this short term trading with the long-term strategy working out for the largest coins by market cap.

Long-term strategy:

With the tax rates in the US, it makes sense to hold onto investments for at least one year due to capital gains tax (which we went over in Chapter 4). If you play it short, you'll need to save enough to cover the additional tax burden. If you play it long, you get to keep more of your earnings provided the coins continue to rise in value.

For the long-term strategy, I prefer to rely upon buying in during the dips in price and holding. As we descend during this rough market, I space out my buys to help lower the average buy-in price. Holding onto your coins and then also adding to your position over time is the best way to traditionally build value as well as increase your wealth in stable stocks.

While coins are not stocks, it's important to think of them as another vehicle for your future wealth.

By holding onto Bitcoin, and other major alternative coins you can hedge with which one becomes the mainstream market go-to after the public use case expands to where crypto-currency becomes more involved in people's regular lives.

This is also very effective because it let's you add to your position over time when the crypto market has its inevitable dips. For example, Bitcoin recently touched $4800 back in August 2017. It then swung downwards, as low as $2800, before starting to climb back up to a $19000 valuation near the peak of 2017. If you were holding during this time, you would not want to cash out, but rather you would be looking to add at the lower prices!

I am a big supporter of the dollar cost averaging/holding strategy for a few reasons:

1.) Crypto-coins have risen in value since 2009
2.) Crypto-coins are gaining acceptance in new markets, not losing it
3.) Crypto-coins continue to adopt new technologies to improve performance and usability

With these three factors, it's apparent that this technology isn't just going to go away on its own.

Your investment reasoning may take into account other variables that I haven't mentioned or even thought of (!) but it's important to note these three for why a holding strategy is less likely to fail long-term than investing in random small coins for example.

It's also important to mention that with institutional investors starting to get into crypto-currency, there will be a flood of money coming in that can raise the market caps and prices very quickly.

It's time for the "past performance does not predict future value" portion of the trading strategy section of this book.

There are risks associated with this. If you only read news headlines, you may have even heard the term "bubble" being thrown around when it comes to Bitcoin, etc. While that ended up being true, it neglects to mention that bubbles are part of a normal market cycle! Look at the stock market for an example of this cycle. Historically, prior to the current bull market run, recessions would occur once every eight years in the U.S. Does that sound like a bubble or a cycle? If you answered both, then you are correct. Did the regular stock market have a bubble with Internet stocks? Did the regular stock market have a bubble in housing stocks? Did the regular stock market have a bubble in tech stocks?

When you look at the boom and bust cycle, there will always be a bubble portion. What people are afraid of is investing, losing everything and then the market never returning. However, let's take a look at a few things:

Could the market cap of crypto all disappear overnight? I'm very confident in saying that's not going to happen. I'd venture to say that's highly unlikely, especially as adoption of these coins as payment platforms continues to increase along with the usage of Bitcoin to be a store of value rises.

Will Bitcoin or crypto be the next Pets.com or the next Amazon? You can decide for yourself, but from where I'm sitting, it looks like money to be had if you get in before the mainstream.

In fact, I might even guarantee that that is the case with crypto-currency. Since it is decentralized, no one government or one entity can come along and kill off the entire market. You would see a massive outpouring of news and have plenty of red flags before the entire blockchain system collapsed. (And this is highly improbable due to how distributed the network truly is).

As with all things related to investments, it's important to view things with the macro lens and not get too caught up in the day-to-day activities that can drive a news cycle.
I have seen people lose a lot of money by playing with market timing and trying to guess which chart predicts where the value of coins will be next.

Due to this, my suggestion for the long term holding strategy is probably the safest one, but there will always be someone claiming to have beat the system with their technique or skill level. It's up to you whether to believe in them or not.

This long-term strategy still includes looking for solid fundamentals, good technical analysis and knowing what problem each coin is attempting to solve.

This is just like investing in the stock of a company. You will want to check in regularly to ensure that your money is being put to good use.

As we've seen with Initial Coin Offerings (remember, ICOs?), there are some real scam coins that exist, so it is up to you to make sure your long-term investments have solid objective reasons behind them. Luckily, the major coins have just that.

Now are you interested in a strategy for day trading crypto-coins? Great! I highly recommend that you follow the appropriate day traders on twitter. I've listed some in the back of this book.

They know far more than I do about that realm and even though they do get things wrong from time to time, there are a lot of people day trading and not needing to work a 9-5 anymore because of how good they've gotten at it.

With crypto-currency, this is a round the clock venture every day of the week. It can make for wild swings based on rumors or news that otherwise wouldn't occur on the stock market. It's important to protect yourself with stop loss limits and also to not overexpose yourself on shorts with this kind of market. I would recommend a more conservative approach with your trading in crypto just because of its inherent volatility. Peaks are greater than normal stocks, but the dips are also deeper.

Be careful!

Chapter 6: Waking Up to Reality

It is December 2018, and we have just witnessed both the extreme highs of cryptocurrency investing as well as the extreme lows. These swings are quite real and while I've described them before, let me put this into numerical context as well as a timeline to show just how extreme it is.

Crypto investing is not for the weak willed and is not for people without patience. That means you cannot have weak hands and you must keep an eye to the long-term trend at all times when going through the bear markets.

On December 17th, 2017, Bitcoin hit its peak at over $19,783 per coin, reaching its peak value of all time as of this writing.

During this frenzied rush to the top (Bitcoin reached this peak over a 3 week period!), alt coins followed in similar fashion, posting the largest investments gains for the year. (For example, Ripple's XRP went from a valuation of $0.0063 on January 1st, to a peak of $2.30 at the end of 2017 – a 36,600% rise in value!)

Ethereum, the popular alternative to Bitcoin for developing blockchain applications (d-apps) and ERC-20 tokens used by many to start their own ICOs, experienced a huge up swell of support with valuation starting at $7 in January 2017 and peaking at the end of the year at $850, a 10,000% gain.

The abundance of ERC-20 tokens and expansion of projects created a bubble backed by euphoria, as gains this large are incredibly historic.

Smelling profits, a lot of celebrities and Internet marketing personalities began to get involved heavily, offering their expertise to new investors on how to navigate this new, exciting wealth creation market.

The party wasn't ending as we headed into January 2018. Large firms were projecting Bitcoin at $50,000 or $60,000 by March 2018. Imagine the newfound wealth from a gamble in new technology driving your perspective to the reward mindset vs. risk over the course of a few weeks.

Then Bitcoin sold off.

At first, people leapt at being able to buy the dip, and then as it continued to fall with alt coins dropping like flies, more and more people left crypto altogether.

Yes, 2018 has been that kind of crazy year where we experienced the highs and the lowest of lows. The majority of investors have left and the prices reflect that.

If you purchased my previous books, you'd know I was a large advocate of HODL and buying the dips in 2017. While that strategy is still sound, it is heavily dependent on two very important things:

1). What your entry price was

2). What an acceptable timeframe for holding is for you.

There is a real opportunity cost associated with blindly holding onto a coin. For example, I personally invested into a coin called Vertcoin (VTC) back when it was 63 cents a coin in 2017. I bought the dips and rode that coin until selling it at $9.21.

For a few short months of holding, a huge profit was made from this. However, if you did not sell during this Bull run and instead chose to hold onto it, your price per coin for VTC as of this writing is only 29 cents.

Did I sell at the peak? No, the peak was over $10 at one point. Was this luck? No.

In the movie Wall Street (classic 1980's film worth seeing if you haven't), there is a saying that rings very true, "Pigs get slaughtered." I think most of the people involved in crypto became pigs during the euphoria stage and a lot of them were slaughtered once Bitcoin crashed.

Now here is the tricky part to this whole experience of rapid market expansion and then collapse: The technology didn't influence the market pricing.

If you're shaking your head right now in agreement, then you know that market cycles are much more a reflection of human psychology than the content itself. As we move forward through the cycle, the human emotional response is very similar each time. Since bubbles are just condensed market cycles, being able to detach yourself from the frenzy or depression as it moves is a talent that will separate you from other investors and traders.

Here is an investing strategy that you should keep in mind while you examine charts. <u>Always pay attention to market sentiment.</u> This is not something to rely solely upon, but rather to keep in the front of your mind as you go through the cycle.

Here are some key indicators of when to sell an asset and when to buy it, in no particular order:

1). When celebrities start getting involved during a market expansion, look to start selling.

2). Once investment courses start to come out and be advertised on social media or TV, look to sell.

3). Once you see the space full of traders that are posting incorrect charts and making price projections, look to sell.

4). Once paid trading groups emerge around a cult of personality, look to sell.

5). Once CNBC starts talking about how amazing an asset is and that you should get involved, look to sell.

Now, how will you know when it's becoming a good time to buy?

1). When all the celebrities have left, it's time to look to start to invest again

2). When all the investment gurus stop advertising and leave the space altogether, look to start to invest again.

3). Once you see the space lacking traders posting charts and only a few are still active on social media at all, look to get invested again.

4). Once the paid trading groups have dramatic shut downs and people are calling for their money back? Laugh and then look to build up a position

5). Once CNBC starts talking about the death of your asset, look to buy.

Amazing how that inverse can work. It is viewed as contrarian, but think for yourself. If making money through investing was as simple as watching CNBC or listening to celebrities, why isn't everyone successful?

This chapter has become much longer than I intended but there is so much to relay to a new investor here during this market. Always stay informed about the market. It allows you to make better decisions with your purchasing, holding and taking of profits when the time comes. It will also let you know which coins are worth investing in, and which to avoid as the Bear market helps to pick winners and losers on it's own.

The problem with investing in crypto has been a separation of this knowledge from the general public so far. Many believe that this was a scam and that it will die off and go away.

This unfortunately will continue to separate the haves from the have-not's further as now is the time to start to seriously begin buying back in.

Please do your friends and family a favor and inform them of this trend to help arm them with the knowledge they will need to get ahead of the game.

The future is bright and the dips are expected. Where else can you go to learn more about the various topics we have discussed in this book in more detail? Well, I've been searching around and have put together some additional resources that you can use, read, share and post about to drive some good conversations around crypto-currency and the market in general. The intent of this list was not to be all-inclusive, but rather to serve up some different areas of knowledge that line up with what we've discussed in this book so far.

The best thing about crypto-currency is that all of the information about it that is relevant can be found on the Internet with a lot of searching.

My intent has been to condense all of that information to save you time as well as provide you with the locations of resources that can help you grow as an investor and crypto-advocate. I did this so that you would be able to learn all of the basics in one place without needlessly sitting in front of a computer for days on end.

Your learning should not stop here and I'm going to provide you with several key resources in the next chapter that will allow you to gain more in-depth information on any of the topics that we have gone over in this book.

The different coins that make up cryptocurrency all have their own support groups, fan clubs and news sites that you can follow. It is important to know what your investments are doing so that you can plan accordingly. Since this is a 24x7x365 market, each week will bring with it a lot of news and headlines about each coin.

Without anymore delay, the chapter which can set you on the path to self-learning…

Chapter 7: Additional Resources

This book was not intended to capture everything surrounding crypto-currency. If you would like to learn more about mining, hard wallets and charts then my 2nd edition is the way to go, albeit with a 2017 growth mindset attached to it.

For a great background on Bitcoin and the origins of it, I would recommend the documentary on Netflix called <u>Banking on Bitcoin</u>. This will give you the story of Satoshi Nakamoto and some theories on who he could have been.

Other resources include:

https://www.cryptoinsider.com

https://www.cryptocoinsnews.com

https://www.coindesk.com

https://news.bitcoin.com

For information on Bitcoin mining, three sites I enjoy are:

https://www.coinish.com

https://www.cryptocompare.com

https://www.bitcoinmining.com

For information on Crypto taxes, here are two sites you should memorize:

https://www.irs.gov/newsroom/irs-virtual-currency-guidance

https://turbotax.intuit.com/tax-tools/tax-tips/Taxes-101/Tax-Tips-for-Bitcoin-and-Virtual-Currency/INF29402.html

For technical analysis information, the site I use is:

https://www.technicallycrypto.com

As always, check the charts and learn to identify patterns.

For fun, I also like to check social media accounts (Twitter especially). This is a collection of users that I personally follow and feel that they help provide positive contributions to the crypto community.

There are literally hundreds of accounts worth mentioning but to keep it short for space purposes, here are some random ones that offer good content.

@DM_BrooksCrypto
@TechnicalCrypto
@CharlieShrem
@CryptoNewsWire
@CryptoPikachu
@NicTrades
@Crypt0maniacs
@chryspto
@etcmining
@Crypto-Tube
@Beerdhead
@RealTimeCrypto
@PrecioBTC

After you follow these accounts, you'll start to see other people suggested and my recommendation is to follow most accounts associated with crypto. You may also find yourself laughing at the latest picture shared among the group above.

It's easy to gain insights and knowledge from the community into what's causing a market rise or dip, and if we are going to make a lot of money soon or just lose it all in one blip. (I'm kidding).

Develop your network with like-minded individuals and you'll eventually get the information you need quicker than the web sites will report it.

This will help you keep a step ahead with your trades, buys and sells. It's not insider trading, but it's definitely an advantage, which you should take full use of in the crypto game!

I wouldn't be where I am now with my crypto portfolio, earnings and other benefits from this journey if it weren't for the vast amount of information already out there and people willing to teach new joiners to the crypto world.

It's important to share the knowledge and pass it on because there is so much upside left to this growing technology.
Don't ever feel like you are limited in what you can accomplish with crypto-currency because like the internet in 1994, no one yet knows where it is going or how it will completely change our lives.

Now head over to Coinbase and let's get started together on this journey to wealth in crypto. Invest as much or as little as you can afford – the amount does not matter right now. You can invest $1 if you want, but it's better to start now rather than waste any more time. The best to build is during a bear market.

Chapter 8: Good Luck!

Thank you for reading this book about crypto-currency and congratulations on learning more about the crypto bear market.

In this book I have attempted to describe at what crypto-currency is, what some of its advantages and disadvantages are, it's use cases, the tax game, the crypto market outlook and lastly my own trading strategy I would recommend for crypto investments.

With that said, there are a lot of details and areas that I have purposefully not discussed in this publication due to the intended audience.

At this point, Bitcoin has received enough media attention that it should be a familiar topic to most people at least in name only.

I highly recommend the 2nd edition of How Anyone Can Invest in Crypto-Currency if you have questions about the mechanics of buying, selling, storing or mining crypto-currency.

Thank you for reading and supporting my writing. I greatly appreciate your support.

If you've enjoyed this book, you would be helping me out tremendously if you left a positive review on Amazon. It supports my writing in the future the more good reviews I receive. If you have found this book to be lacking in areas or wish to critique it, please send me an email at **CryptoBrooks@gmail.com** I welcome any and all feedback as it only makes my writing better.

I would like to thank my wife Sara, my dog Mario, Schmoe the cat for providing support for the time commitment.

A thank you Reddit, Google, Twitter, CNN, NY Times, Bloomberg, MSNBC and any other site that has run headlines in the mainstream news about alt coins and crypto-currency. You've made me a lot of money by saying the wrong things consistently.

If you would like to donate Bitcoin to help me prepare for another book, you can send it to my address listed on the next page or scan the code.

1C4gZQivPfujSzdqqYcT7hKnz8LEUFXSpC

Any and all donations are greatly appreciated.

To those venturing out into investing in crypto after reading this, Good Luck! You will make some money if you practice patience!

 Thank you!

- D.M.Brooks

Works Cited

Chapter 1:

Zimbabwe 100 Trillion Dollars photo
http://www.CNN.com. Accessed 25 July 2017.

Bitcoin price over time photo
https://99bitcoins.com/price-chart-history/
Accessed 27 September 2017.

Chapter 2:

Blockchain
https://en.wikipedia.org/wiki/Blockchain.
Accessed 25 July 2017.

JP Morgan's Dimon says "Bitcoin is a Fraud"
https://www.reuters.com/article/legal-us-usa-banks-conference-jpmorgan/jpmorgans-dimon-says-bitcoin-is-a-fraud-idUSKCN1BN2PN Accessed 28 September 2017.

Chapter 3:

Technological Growth Curve chart from:
Crossing the Chasm, Geoffrey A. Moore 3rd Edition 2014
Google Images for the chart, accessed 23 September, 2017

Chapter 4:

IRS rules from IRS.Gov
https://www.irs.gov/newsroom/irs-virtual-currency-guidance

Additional tax information courtesy of Turbo Tax
https://turbotax.intuit.com/tax-tools/tax-tips/Taxes-101/Tax-Tips-for-Bitcoin-and-Virtual-Currency/INF29402.html

Chapter 5:

Bitcoin prices over time chart. Money Minded.
https://www.facebook.com/permalink.php?id=1951736161706253&story_fbid=1953020834911119 Accessed 26 July 2017.

www.ingramcontent.com/pod-product-compliance
Lightning Source LLC
Chambersburg PA
CBHW060901170526
45158CB00001B/442